LIVING LEGENDS OF SPORTS

CALVIN "MEGATRON" JOHNSON
SUPERSTAR WIDE RECEIVER

SIMONE PAYMENT

Britannica Educational Publishing
IN ASSOCIATION WITH
ROSEN
EDUCATIONAL SERVICES

I0869314

Published in 2019 by Britannica Educational Publishing (a trademark of Encyclopædia Britannica, Inc.) in association with The Rosen Publishing Group, Inc.
29 East 21st Street, New York, NY 10010

Distributed exclusively by Rosen Publishing.
To see additional Britannica Educational Publishing titles, go to rosenpublishing.com.

First Edition

Britannica Educational Publishing
J.E. Luebering: Executive Director, Core Editorial
Andrea R. Field: Managing Editor, Compton's by Britannica

Rosen Publishing
Kathy Kuhtz Campbell: Senior Editor
Nicole Russo-Duca: Series Designer and Book Layout
Cindy Reiman: Photography Manager
Sherri Jackson: Photo Researcher

Library of Congress Cataloging-in-Publication Data

Names: Payment, Simone author.
Title: Calvin "Megatron" Johnson : superstar wide receiver / Simone Payment.
Description: First Edition. | New York: Britannica Educational Publishing, in Association with Rosen Educational Services, 2019. | Series: Living Legends of Sports | Includes bibliographical references and index. | Audience: Grades: 5–8.
Identifiers: LCCN 2018011883| ISBN 9781508106319 (library bound) | ISBN 9781508106302 (paperback)
Subjects: LCSH: Johnson, Calvin, 1985—Juvenile literature. | Football players—United States—Biography—Juvenile literature. | Detroit Lions (Football team)—History—Juvenile literature.
Classification: LCC GV939.J6123 P38 2019 | DDC 796.332092 [B] —dc23
LC record available at https://lccn.loc.gov/2018011883

Manufactured in the United States of America

Photo credits: Cover Dave Reginek/Getty Images; back cover, p. 3 and interior pages (football field chalk drawing) © iStockphoto.com /Traffic Analyzer; pp. 4-5, 30-31 Gregory Shamus/Getty Images; pp. 7, 15, 26 David Bergman/Sports Illustrated/Getty Images; pp. 9, 17, 22-23, 27, 33, 34 © AP mages; p. 10 Grant Halverson/Getty Images; p. 11 Bob Rosato/Sports Illustrated/Getty Images; p. 12 Rob Tringali/SportsChrome /Getty Images; pp. 18-19 Bruce Gordon/UPI/Newscom; p. 21 The Sporting News/Getty Images; p. 25 Simon Bruty/Sports Illustrated/Getty Images; p. 29 Fort Worth Star-Telegram/Tribune News Service/Getty Images; p. 35 D Dipasupil/FilmMagic /Getty Images; p. 37 Kathy Hutchins/Shutterstock.com; p. 39 Ron Elkman/Sports Imagery/Getty Images.

CONTENTS

INTRO-DUCTION

Calvin "Megatron" Johnson was a football star almost from the first day he stepped on the field. His height, speed, and ability to make acrobatic leaps and catches made him one of the best wide receivers ever to play the game. Johnson spent nine seasons in the National Football League (NFL), from 2007 to 2015. He played all nine of those seasons with the Detroit Lions. During his NFL career he scored 83 touchdowns. He made 731 receptions for an amazing total of 11,619 yards.

Johnson impressed fans, coaches, teammates, and players on opposing teams. Often people could not believe how fast he was. He ran past defenders as if they were standing still. Sometimes the catches he made seemed impossible. He would leap to incredible heights, twisting his body at the same time to make a catch. James Lofton, an NFL radio analyst, told Austin Murphy of *Sports Illustrated*: "Everybody knows they're throwing [Johnson] the ball, and he catches it anyway."

Off the field, Johnson worked as hard as he could to make the most of his speed and abilities. Every day of the week he prepared so he would be able to perform well on game days. As amazing as he was, he never called any attention to himself. He preferred to stay out of the media spotlight and let his performance on the field speak for him.

Calvin Johnson makes one of his typically acrobatic catches to score a touchdown in a September 2014 game against the New York Giants.

CHAPTER ONE

A Head Above Right from the Beginning

Calvin Johnson Jr. was born in Newnan, Georgia, on September 29, 1985. Newnan is about 40 miles southwest of Atlanta, Georgia. His father, Calvin Johnson Sr., was a train conductor for the Southern Pacific Railroad. Johnson's mother, Arica, worked for the Atlanta public school system. Johnson has an older sister named Erica. He also has a younger brother, Wali, and a younger sister, Elan. When Calvin was still a boy, the family moved to Tyrone, about 25 miles southwest of Atlanta.

The Johnsons were a close-knit family. They went to church together on Sundays. Johnson's parents emphasized that it was important to be a good person. Johnson was very kind as a child. His mother told Austin Murphy the advice she gave her son: "If you treat people the way you want to be treated, things will work out." Both of Johnson's parents taught their children the importance of hard work and of doing a job well. Johnson's mother also stressed that education was very important. As Johnson told Murphy, "You didn't want to bring home anything but an A or a B. To my mom, a C was like an F." Johnson wanted to please his parents and always tried his best to get good grades.

Calvin Johnson's family attended the 2007 NFL Draft with him. From left to right are his father, Calvin Sr.; Calvin Jr.; his sisters, Erica and Elan; his mother, Arica; and his brother, Wali.

Sports, Sports, Sports

Growing up, Johnson loved sports. He loved watching them as much as he loved playing them. He was a big fan of the Atlanta Braves baseball team. He played Little League baseball starting when he was five or six. He played outfield and catcher, and sometimes pitched.

Johnson also loved football. But, when he was in elementary school and junior high school, his mother would not allow him to play the sport. She believed football was too dangerous.

QUICK FACT

Johnson looked up to Ken Griffey Jr., an outfielder for the Seattle Mariners, Cincinnati Reds, and Chicago White Sox.

By the time Johnson was 12 years old, he was already 6 feet tall. His height gave him an advantage in sports.

When Johnson started at Sandy Creek High School in Tyrone, his mother decided to allow him to play football. He joined his high school's team, the Patriots, playing wide receiver. He took the number 81.

Even though Johnson had just started playing football, it did not take him long to catch on. By his sophomore year he had grown to be 6 feet, 4 inches. He became the starting wide receiver. Before long, he was considered one of the best high school football players in Georgia.

QUICK FACT

The job of a wide receiver is to catch the ball thrown by the quarterback. The wide receiver then attempts to get the ball into the end zone to score a touchdown.

Johnson's speed is part of what made him such a good wide receiver. His ability to jump very high to catch the ball was another advantage. He was also able to make acrobatic leaps and catches very few other people could make. Chip Walker, his coach in high school, remembers one such amazing play by Johnson. Walker told Austin Murphy that Johnson "knock[ed] the cornerback into two other guys [taking out] all three of 'em."

College Superstar

Johnson chose to go to Georgia Tech for college and play for its football team, the Yellow Jackets. Getting a good education was important to Johnson and his family, so Georgia Tech was a good choice. Also, it is in Atlanta, so Johnson would not be far from home. Johnson decided to major in building construction.

Johnson made a mark at Georgia Tech even before his first football season started in the fall of 2004. During training camp he broke school records. One record he broke was how high he could jump—43 inches. Another was how far he could jump from a standing position—11 feet 3 inches. Johnson was now 6 feet 5 inches

Chip Walker, Johnson's high school football coach, won three Georgia state championships with Sandy Creek High School, including this 2009 win at the Georgia Dome in Atlanta.

tall. He wore number 21 on his jersey at Georgia Tech.

In one of Johnson's first games with the Yellow Jackets, he scored the winning touchdown against Clemson. He jumped over the defender to make the catch in the end zone. Johnson immediately impressed his coaches and teammates and the players on opposing teams. However, he was always trying to improve. In an

QUICK FACT

Several colleges with excellent football teams recruited Johnson to come play for them. Some of the top teams included the University of Notre Dame and the University of Miami.

October game against the Miami Hurricanes, Johnson made only two catches. Years later, Johnson looked back on that game. He told Austin Murphy that game had made him realize that he was "going to have to work harder, get stronger and improve my technique a lot."

Johnson already worked hard to improve his skills, but he began to work even harder. Buddy Geis, who coached the receivers on the team, noticed Johnson's efforts. Geis told Mark Beech of *Sports Illustrated* that Johnson was "so talented, but he also outworks a lot of our older kids ... Whatever you tell him, he does it right and at full speed. He's improving all the time."

Johnson made this terrific catch for a touchdown in a September 2004 game against the Clemson Tigers. Johnson and his Georgia Tech teammates won the game 28–24.

Johnson's hard work paid off. In the fourth quarter of a November game against North Carolina State, Johnson caught a pass with one hand. Marcus Hudson, who played for the other team, compared the catch to something Spider-Man might be able to do. Johnson's teammates began calling him "Spider-Man." They also called him "Neo" after the character Keanu Reeves plays in the movie *The Matrix*.

Despite his amazing plays, Johnson did not celebrate after scoring touchdowns like some other players do. He simply set the football down on the field. Eventually some of his teammates convinced him to do something to celebrate. But they could not get him to do much more than give his teammates a high five.

Johnson studied hard and did well in his college classes. On and off the field he was quiet and serious.

By the end of Johnson's freshman year, he had made 48 catches for 837 yards. He scored seven touchdowns that year. As a sophomore Johnson continued to succeed. That year he had 54 catches for 888 yards and scored six touchdowns.

During the summer after his sophomore year, Johnson worked on a project to design solar-powered latrines. He later went to Bolivia to help build the latrines he had designed.

In his junior year, 2006, Johnson was even more of a standout player. He made 76 catches and

Johnson scored a touchdown in the first game of the 2006 season against the University of Notre Dame. That year he helped Georgia Tech reach the Atlantic Coast Conference (ACC) Championship Game.

Johnson makes a spectacular catch against the Virginia Tech Hokies in 2006, helping Georgia Tech to a 38–27 win.

scored 15 touchdowns, which was a Georgia Tech record. He had an impressive 1,202 receiving yards, breaking another school record. That year he won the Fred Biletnikoff Award as the best college wide receiver in the United States.

Johnson's head coach at Georgia Tech, Chan Gailey, was sure he would be a star in the NFL. Gailey believed Johnson would be a superstar because of his great talent. But he also knew Johnson would succeed because of all the hard work he put into improving his skills.

QUICK FACT

Georgia Tech's sports teams play in the Atlantic Coast Conference (ACC). Johnson was the first Georgia Tech player to earn first-team All-ACC honors three times.

CHAPTER TWO

Lion Cub

Calvin Johnson had a decision to make following his third year at Georgia Tech. Many people believed he could become an extremely successful player in the NFL. If Johnson entered the NFL Draft, he was sure to be signed to a high-paying deal. He had to decide whether to go to college one more year to complete his degree or to leave school and become a professional football player. Education was important to Johnson and his family. But Johnson decided that his last year of college could wait until after his football career. He entered the 2007 NFL Draft.

Drafted!

The Detroit Lions were one of the worst teams in the NFL. They had won only three games in the 2006 football season. Because of their poor record, they had the chance to make the second pick in the 2007 NFL Draft. They chose Johnson. Lions fans watching the draft on television at Ford Field, the team's home stadium, went wild with excitement. They believed Johnson could help turn their team around. Some fans were worried that the Lions would trade Johnson to another team. But the Lions kept Johnson and offered him a six-year, $64 million deal to play for them.

The 2007 NFL Draft took place at Radio City Music Hall in New York City. Johnson shows off his jersey after being picked second by the Detroit Lions.

QUICK FACT

At the time of his signing, Johnson was the highest paid player ever for the Lions. He held that title until quarterback Matthew Stafford signed a contract extension with the Lions in 2017 for $135 million.

Over the summer of 2007 Johnson and the Lions worked out the details of his contract. The contract negotiations made Johnson nervous. He just wanted to get to work preparing for the upcoming football season. Finally, on August 3, Johnson signed his contract and made it official: he was now a Detroit Lion. On his jersey, he chose to wear his high school number, 81. The same day he signed the contract, practice started at 8:30 a.m. and Johnson was on the field ready to work.

Even before his contract was signed, Johnson had begun working out with his teammates. They were already very impressed with his many talents. They were equally impressed with how hard he worked. Mike Furrey, another receiver on the team, told Larry Lage of the Associated Press that fans were "excited about Calvin, but they don't even know what they've got yet. He's going to be one of the top receivers in the league in a couple years."

Off to a Good Start, But ...

Johnson's first NFL game was against the Oakland Raiders, on September 9, 2007. It did not take him long to make an impact. In the third quarter of the game, Johnson scored his first NFL touchdown. After scoring, Johnson just put the ball down on the field. His teammate Roy Williams, another wide receiver, picked up the ball and gave it to Johnson. He thought Johnson might want to save it as a reminder of his first professional touchdown. The Lions went on to win that game 36–21. They won their second game as well.

Early in the season, Johnson injured his back. He continued playing anyway and did well even though he was injured. But overall the Lions season was not very good. In fact, in the second half of the season, the team lost six games in a row.

Months before they signed Johnson, the Lions invited him to their minicamp in May 2007. Johnson worked out with the team at its training facility in Allen Park, Michigan.

Johnson later admitted to the *Players' Tribune* that he was nervous in his first professional game, but he was all smiles on the sidelines after making his first NFL touchdown.

Johnson was well prepared for his professional career on the field. He was very shy, though, when it came to another part of the job: talking to reporters. Johnson was very polite but would not say much more than "yes" or "no" in response to their questions.

QUICK FACT

During Johnson's first season, his teammate Roy Williams nicknamed him "Megatron" after the character from the Transformers comics and movies. Williams chose the nickname because of Johnson's size. Because of Johnson's speed, some of his teammates also called him "Bolt" after track star and Olympic gold medalist Usain Bolt.

At the end of his first professional season, Johnson looked back on what he had accomplished. Although he had played well, he believed he could play even better. Johnson thought he was not making the most of his talents. He decided he would work even harder in the 2008 season. Johnson set a goal for himself of at least 100 receiving yards per game. He believed that was a realistic goal and one that he could reach or beat each week.

To prepare for the 2008 season, Johnson worked hard on all his skills. He had always been fast, but he did not think he was fast enough. He thought that if he could cut corners while running he would be even faster. But he had to be in control at the same time so he would not slip. Johnson did all kinds of drills to improve his footwork. He ran through a series of cones or through ladders laid flat on the ground. He dribbled soccer balls around with the other receivers.

QUICK FACT

The 2008 Detroit Lions were the first team in NFL history to lose all 16 games of the season. In 2017, the Cleveland Browns joined them as the only other team to go 0–16.

Johnson also wanted to improve his "take-off" and stay low to the ground when he started running. This approach would make him a smaller target for other players, making it harder for them to defend against him. Shawn Jefferson, the Lions receivers coach, made him take off by running underneath a pipe that was set at waist level.

Despite all of Johnson's hard work and preparations, 2008 was a terrible season for the Lions. In fact, the Lions lost every single game that year. The one bright spot to the season was that Johnson had 12 touchdowns. He tied Larry Fitzgerald of the Arizona Cardinals for the most receiving touchdowns in the NFL.

Starting to Turn It Around

After the disaster of the 2008 season, the Lions made some changes. They hired all new coaches. They also signed Matthew Stafford from the University of Georgia as their new quarterback. Stafford and Johnson were very much alike. They had a similar attitude and personality. They communicated well on the field. Johnson and Stafford became good friends.

Johnson's speed, agility, and great catches were not enough to get the Lions past any of their 2008 opponents. One problem the Lions had that season was injuries to their quarterbacks.

Johnson and quarterback Matthew Stafford (*left*) celebrate after Stafford threw a touchdown pass to Johnson in an October 2010 game against the Washington Redskins. The Lions won by the score of 37–25.

Despite the changes the Lions made to players and coaches, the 2009 season was only a little better than the previous one. The Lions won just two games the whole season. It was not Johnson's best season either. He scored just five touchdowns and had 984 receiving yards, down from 1,331 yards the year before.

The 2010 season was better for Johnson and the Lions. They still did not have a good season, winning just six games out of 16. But Johnson improved his touchdown count to 12 and finished with 1,120 receiving yards. He and Stafford were working well together, and Lions fans hoped the team was heading in the right direction.

CHAPTER THREE

Pride of the Lions

In the 2011 season, the Lions did turn things around. For the first time in his career as a Lion, Johnson got to end a season with a winning record. The Lions won 10 of their 16 games. And, in another first for Johnson as a Lion, the team made the National Football Conference playoffs as a wild card. Although they lost to the New Orleans Saints in their playoff game, a winning season was certainly an improvement.

Whether the Lions were winning or not, Johnson continued to impress his teammates and Lions fans. In a game against the Carolina Panthers on November 20, 2011, Stafford passed to Johnson and his throw was too high. Johnson jumped for it, twisting his body to make the catch. Looking back on the game, Stafford told Austin Murphy of *Sports Illustrated* that Johnson "made it look so easy, when probably nobody else in the league even jumps for it." Johnson finished the 2011 regular season with a career high of 16 touchdowns. He had 96 receptions, the most he had had to that point in his career. His total of 1,681 receiving yards was the best in the NFL.

Johnson leapt to catch a pass but failed to snag it in the 2011 National Football Conference playoffs against the New Orleans Saints. However, he did catch 12 passes for two touchdowns in the game.

A Standout Season

Johnson signed a contract extension in 2012 to stay with the Lions. The Lions loved having Johnson as a player. He performed well on the field and worked hard. He never got into any trouble off the field. The Lions were eager to keep him with the team and were willing to pay him to stay. His contract extension was worth $132 million. After Johnson signed the contract, the Lions held a news conference. Johnson spoke to reporters and then went back to the

QUICK FACT

In April 2012, Johnson won a fan vote to be on the cover of the *Madden NFL 13* video game. Panthers quarterback Cam Newton was the runner-up.

Johnson had many reasons to smile in 2012, including a contract extension and record-breaking statistics.

room where he had signed the contract. Before going to practice, he straightened up the room. He put all the chairs back where they had been before the meeting.

Johnson injured his knee, ankle, foot, and hands during the 2012 season. None of these injuries seemed to slow him down. He performed so well that sportswriters started talking about the possibility of Johnson reaching 2,000 receiving yards that season. In 1995, Jerry Rice had set the single-season NFL record with 1,848 receiving yards. Reporters had often compared Johnson to Rice. Some said Johnson was even better than Rice. That was because Johnson could do things that Rice could not, like leap high in the air.

Reporters asked Johnson about breaking Rice's record or going even higher and hitting 2,000 receiving yards. Johnson thought it was possible. He said it was not the main thing he thought about, though.

Johnson celebrates with his dad after breaking Jerry Rice's single-season receiving yards record in a December 2012 game against his hometown Atlanta Falcons.

Instead, he focused on the many things he did to prepare himself to perform well on the field each week. He told *Sports Illustrated* that he did not think too far ahead or worry about how people would think of him in the future. He said he was "more of a day-to-day guy. There are so many little things to do now."

Despite all the injuries, Johnson had a personal best and league-leading 122 receptions in 2012. And he broke another record. He surged past Rice's record with an amazing 1,964 receiving yards. Johnson accomplished this personal record while his team as a whole did not perform well. The Lions won just four games that season.

More Personal Excellence

QUICK FACT

Although Julio Jones of the Atlanta Falcons came close to Johnson's record with 1,871 receiving yards in 2015, Johnson still held the single-season record for most receiving yards heading into the 2018 season.

The 2013 season was another excellent one for Johnson. By the end of the season he had scored 12 touchdowns. He had another impressive total of receiving yards—this time, 1,492. That meant that over the 2011, 2012, and 2013 seasons he compiled 5,137 receiving yards. That number was the most in the NFL over those years by far. He had 1,120 more yards than Brandon Marshall, the next closest player.

Johnson continued to dazzle fans, coaches, and other players with his size, speed, and acrobatic plays. Seattle Seahawks cornerback Richard Sherman talked to *Sports Illustrated* about Johnson. He explained that Johnson was "faster than you think ... Taller and stronger than you think ... Calvin's playing ball at a different level from anyone else." Sherman was amazed that even with three or four defenders trying to cover Johnson, somehow he would make the catch or score the touchdown anyway.

Once again, though, the Lions had a losing season in 2013, winning seven games but losing nine. In 2014, things improved for the

Johnson always impressed fans, players, and coaches with his ability to jump higher than his opponents. In this 2013 game he towered above two Dallas Cowboys defenders.

Just out of reach of Philadelphia Eagles' defensive back Malcolm Jenkins, Johnson catches one of his three touchdowns in a 45–14 Lions win in November 2015.

team. The Lions won 11 of their 16 games in the regular season and made the playoffs. However, they lost the Wild Card Game to the Dallas Cowboys and were eliminated from the playoffs.

QUICK FACT

During the 2014 season, Johnson set another record. During the Lions' 34–17 win over the Chicago Bears on Thanksgiving Day, he surpassed 10,000 receiving yards for his career. Johnson had reached that milestone faster than any other player in NFL history.

Johnson turned in another good personal season in 2015. He racked up 1,214 receiving yards and scored nine touchdowns. But the Lions returned to their losing ways, winning just seven games. Johnson was still working hard to prepare each week. He was doing not only football drills, but also many other things to get his body ready to play. He did yoga and got massages. Despite still performing well on the field, Johnson was beginning to look ahead to the future. Was there something out there for Johnson beyond the football field?

CHAPTER FOUR

Off the Field

After the 2015 season, Johnson began to think seriously about retiring from football. By the end of most seasons, Johnson had been in pain from injuries and constant practices and games. In an essay in *The Players' Tribune*, Johnson explained that during the season he had been "in some sort of pain every day." He rarely complained because "what good would that do? It wouldn't make [him] hurt any less. It would just sound like an excuse." So Johnson continued to work hard and play the game as best as he could. But, eventually, Johnson thought his body could not take any more, so he decided to retire.

Johnson did not want to make a big announcement about his decision. He did not hold a press conference. Instead, he posted a statement on the Lions' website. Johnson said that he had decided "to retire from the Lions and pro football." Although it was not an easy decision, he "truly [was] at peace with it." Johnson spent much of his statement thanking his family, his teammates and coaches, the Lions' owners, and the Lions' fans. He finished by saying that he had "loved playing in Detroit and [would] forever be a Lion."

Marriage and Family

During Johnson's playing career, he had little time for anything other than football. He was always working out, practicing, or doing other things to prepare for each game, even in the offseason. He said in his

Players' Tribune essay that if you want to be the best you can be in professional sports, "you have to be selfish." Johnson had always thought he would not be able to spend enough time with his family if he got married. So, he decided to wait until after he retired to get married.

Johnson played his last home game at Ford Field in Detroit on December 27, 2015. After the season ended, Johnson decided to retire.

Calvin's wife, Brittney McNorton Johnson, is a manager in the Lions' promotion department. She and Calvin live part of the year in Michigan.

Johnson married Brittney McNorton in Detroit in June 2016. Johnson had met Brittney while she was working for the Lions as promotions manager. Brittney's father, Bruce, had played cornerback for the Lions in the 1980s so she had grown up around football. Brittney continues to work for the Lions.

QUICK FACT

Johnson has a son, Caleb, from a previous relationship.

Calvin Johnson Jr. Foundation

Early in his football career, Johnson started the Calvin Johnson Jr. Foundation. He wanted to use the foundation to give back to the community in his hometown of Atlanta and in his football home of Detroit. He hoped to help kids in particular and chose the motto "Catching Dreams." Johnson set up the foundation in 2008.

Johnson and actors Julianna Margulies (*center*) and Yara Shahidi (*right*) spoke at the 2016 College Signing Day event in New York City. All three encouraged high school students to continue their education.

The Calvin Johnson Jr. Foundation hosts football camps and provides scholarships for student-athletes. It helps needy families by providing food and hosting toy drives at Christmas. The foundation gives money to teachers to help in their classrooms. It also funds breast cancer research.

QUICK FACT

Johnson donates the money he makes on endorsement deals to the Calvin Johnson Jr. Foundation.

Johnson's mother and sister help run the foundation. While Johnson was playing football, he did not have as much time as he would have liked to work with the foundation. He was very involved in making decisions about the foundation but could not take part in many activities and programs during the football season. One benefit of being retired was that he could spend much more time working to make a difference in other people's lives.

Dancing with the Stars

Less than a year after Johnson retired, producers from the television program *Dancing with the Stars* (*DWTS*) called to ask him to be a contestant. On the show, professional dancers teach actors, professional athletes, and other celebrities how to dance. Then they dance together on the show each week, competing against other teams. Johnson had no dancing experience, so he turned them down. When they called a second time, Johnson's wife encouraged him to give it a try. Johnson decided to go for it.

On his first day of rehearsal for the show, Johnson's dancing partner, Lindsay Arnold Cusick, taught him some easy dance steps. Johnson thought he would do just fine. But as the dance steps got harder, Johnson realized he had a lot of work to do. He approached dancing on *DWTS* just like he had approached playing football. He trained hard every day. He watched videos of his performances to see where he could improve. Johnson worked so hard preparing for the show that he lost 12 pounds.

Johnson and his dancing partner, Lindsay Arnold Cusick, made it to the finale of *Dancing with the Stars* but finished third, behind gymnast Laurie Hernandez and race car driver James Hinchcliffe.

At the first live show, Johnson had a little stage fright. The audience was so close to the stage, and he thought about how many millions of people would be watching him on television. But Johnson went out on the dance floor and did what he had to do. He and Lindsay were a successful partnership. They finished the season in third place. Johnson was glad that he had participated in the show. He wrote in the *Players' Tribune*: "I did things I never thought I would, and I met people I never thought I'd meet."

Plans for the Future

Now that Johnson is retired, he has time to do things he never got to do before. He has tried many new hobbies, including learning to ski and surf. He goes paddle boarding, fishing, and golfing. Johnson is also an excellent table tennis player.

Although it is fun for Johnson to participate in new sports and hobbies, he has plenty of more serious work keeping him busy. Johnson plans to go back to college to complete his bachelor's degree in building construction at Georgia Tech. He spends a good deal of time doing work with his foundation. Johnson has also traveled around the country to work with wide receivers. He has trained players in high school, college, and in the NFL. Johnson teaches the players about the game of football, and he gives lessons in what it takes to play professionally. He also tries to teach the players how to be good people. He considers himself "a cross between a trainer, life coach and educator."

QUICK FACT

In 2018, Johnson was inducted into the College Football Hall of Fame with 12 other former players and coaches.

Johnson does not miss playing professional football or the injuries and endless preparation. He does miss his Lions' teammates and keeps in touch with quarterback Matthew Stafford and other players. He misses his coaches and the Detroit fans.

At the invitation of Miami Dolphins' wide receivers coach Shawn Jefferson, Johnson worked with receivers at the Dolphins' training camp in August 2017.

A big chunk of Johnson's life was dedicated to the game of football. Being a football player was always the biggest part of who Johnson was. Now Johnson has a chance to be "many other things," as he wrote in *The Players' Tribune*. "I'm a husband and a father, a friend, a coach, a mentor and an entrepreneur."

TIMELINE

1985: Calvin Johnson Jr. is born on September 29 in Newnan, Georgia.

2004: Johnson graduates from Sandy Creek High School and begins his first season playing for the Georgia Tech Yellow Jackets.

2006: Johnson wins the Fred Biletnikoff Award as the best college receiver in the United States.

2007: On April 28, Johnson is drafted by the Detroit Lions. On August 3, he signs a contract for six years and $64 million. He plays his first NFL season, finishing with four touchdowns (TDs), 48 receptions, and 756 receiving yards.

2008: Johnson sets up the Calvin Johnson Jr. Foundation. He plays his second season, finishing with 12 TDs, 78 receptions, and 1,331 receiving yards. The Lions become the first NFL team to lose every game of the season.

2009: Johnson plays his third season, finishing with five TDs, 67 receptions, and 984 receiving yards.

2010: Johnson wins the Detroit Lions Good Guy Award from the Detroit media. He plays his fourth season, finishing with 12 TDs, 77 receptions, and 1,120 receiving yards.

2011: The Lions make the playoffs but lose to the New Orleans Saints. Johnson finishes his fifth season with 16 TDs, 96 receptions, and 1,681 receiving yards.

2012: Johnson signs a contract extension with the Lions. He breaks Jerry Rice's single-season NFL record with 1,964 receiving yards. He makes 122 receptions and scores five TDs.

2013: Johnson plays his seventh season with the Lions, finishing with 12 TDs, 84 receptions, and 1,492 receiving yards.

2014: Johnson surpasses 10,000 career receiving yards in a Thanksgiving Day game. The Lions make the playoffs but lose to the Dallas Cowboys. Johnson finishes the season with eight TDs, 71 receptions, and 1,077 receiving yards.

2015: Johnson plays his last season with the Lions, finishing with nine TDs, 88 receptions, and 1,214 receiving yards.

2016: On March 8, Johnson retires from football. In June, he marries Brittney McNorton. He competes on *Dancing with the Stars*, coming in third.

2018: Johnson is inducted into the College Football Hall of Fame.

OTHER LIVING LEGENDS OF FOOTBALL

Jerry Rice (1962–) is considered by many people to be the greatest wide receiver in the history of the NFL. Playing primarily for the San Francisco 49ers, he set NFL records for career touchdowns (208), receptions (1,549), and reception yardage (22,895).

Randy Moss (1977–) was a wide receiver who broke Jerry Rice's record for single-season touchdowns (23) and set an NFL record for most touchdowns in a rookie season (17). He had the most receiving touchdowns in five NFL seasons (1998, 2000, 2003, 2007, and 2009).

Tom Brady (1977–) led the New England Patriots as their quarterback to five Super Bowl victories (2002, 2004, 2005, 2015, and 2017) and was named the game's Most Valuable Player (MVP) four times (2002, 2004, 2015, and 2017). In Super Bowl LII, in February 2018, Brady shattered the record for passing yards in a Super Bowl with 505 yards, breaking the record he had set in Super Bowl LI (466) in 2017.

Drew Brees (1979–) is a quarterback for the New Orleans Saints. He helped the team win its first Super Bowl championship in 2010 and was named that game's MVP. He has had five seasons with more than 5,000 passing yards. As of the end of the 2017 season, he was third (after Peyton Manning and Brett Favre) on the list of passing yard leaders in NFL history with 70,445 yards.

Aaron Rodgers (1983–) is a quarterback for the Green Bay Packers. He led the team to a 31–25 victory over the Pittsburgh Steelers in Super Bowl XLV in 2011 and was selected as the game's MVP. He was only the fourth quarterback in Super Bowl history to pass for more than 300 yards and at least three touchdowns.

Antonio Brown (1988–) has been a wide receiver for the Pittsburgh Steelers since 2010. He has led the NFL in receptions twice (2014 and 2015) and in receiving yards twice (2014 and 2017).

Julio Jones (1989–) has been a wide receiver for the Atlanta Falcons since 2011. He was a first team All-Pro in 2015 and 2016. Jones helped the Falcons win the 2016 NFC championship and advance to Super Bowl LI, which the Falcons lost to the Patriots. He was voted by the players themselves as being number three on the 2017 NFL Top 100 players list. In the 2017 season he was named to his fifth Pro Bowl.

GLOSSARY

bachelor's degree A college degree obtained after four years of study.
conductor A person who operates a train.
contract A legal agreement between two parties.
draft The process of choosing players to join a team.
endorsement deal An agreement to advertise a product or service.
entrepreneur Someone who starts a business or company.
essay A short written work giving a personal view on a subject.
footwork Movement of the feet.
foundation An organization supported by donations.
latrine A toilet, usually outdoors.
life coach An adviser who helps people make decisions, set and reach goals, or deal with problems.
major To choose a specialized subject of study.
press conference A meeting where reporters interview one or more people.
producer A person who supervises a television show.
professional A player who is paid to play a sport.
promotions manager A person who plans programs to generate interest in a football team.
recruit To try to get as a new member or player.
stage fright Nervousness about appearing in front of an audience.
wide receiver A football player who plays offense and is usually the fastest on the team.
wild card A team that does not win its division but still makes the playoffs on the basis of its record.
yoga A system of mind and body exercises.

FOR MORE INFORMATION

Books

Bryant, Howard. *Legends: The Best Players, Games, and Teams in Football*. New York, NY: Puffin Books, 2016.

Edwards, Ethan. *Meet Calvin Johnson: Football's Megatron*. New York, NY: PowerKids Press, 2014.

Fishman, Jon M. *Antonio Brown*. Minneapolis, MN: Lerner Publications Company, 2018.

Frederick, Shane. *Football: The Math of the Game*. North Mankato, MN: Capstone Press, 2012.

Gigliotti, Jim. *The Pro Football Draft*. Broomall, PA: Mason Crest, 2017.

Gramling, Gary. *The Football Fanbook*. New York, NY: Liberty Street, 2017.

Green, Tim. *Touchdown Kid*. New York, NY: Harper, 2017.

Lyon, Drew. *A Superfan's Guide to Pro Football Teams*. North Mankato, MN: Capstone Press, 2018.

Morey, Allan. *The Detroit Lions Story*. Minneapolis, MN: Bellwether Media, 2017.

Nagelhout, Ryan. *The Science of Football*. New York, NY: PowerKids Press, 2016.

Rivkin, Jennifer. *Gridiron Greats: Heroes of Football*. New York, NY: Crabtree Publishing, 2016.

Savage, Jeff. *Calvin Johnson*. Minneapolis, MN: Lerner Publications Company, 2013.

Savage, Jeff. *Tom Brady*. 2nd rev. ed. Minneapolis, MN: Lerner Publications Company, 2015.

Sports Illustrated Kids. *Football: Then to Wow!* New York, NY: Time Home Entertainment, 2014.

Van Pelt, Don, and Brian Wingate. *An Insider's Guide to Football*. New York, NY: Rosen Central, 2015.

Websites

Calvin Johnson Jr. Foundation, Inc.
http://calvinjohnsonjrfoundation.org/

Detroit Lions
http://www.detroitlions.com/

ESPN
http://www.espn.com/nfl/player/stats/_/id/10447/calvin-johnson

Georgia Tech Sports
http://www.ramblinwreck.com/sports/m-footbl/mtt/calvin_johnson_168417.html

National Football League
http://www.nfl.com/player/calvinjohnson/2495647/careerstats

INDEX